Bringing EFT into Schools

A guide for Practitioners

Emotional Freedom is the basis of ALL foundations for learning. This manual gives practitioners the knowledge needed to effectively bring EFT into educational establishments.

Anne Unsworth

6/5/2011

Bringing EFT into Schools

A guide for Practitioners

Emotional Freedom is the basis of ALL foundations for learning.

This manual gives practitioners the knowledge needed to effectively bring EFT into educational establishments.

AuthorHouse™
1663 Liberty Drive
Bloomington, IN 47403
www.authorhouse.com
Phone: 1-800-839-8640

First published by AuthorHouse 06/22/2011

ISBN: 978-1-4567-8409-6 (sc)

authorHOUSE®

Bringing EFT into Schools

Introduction

Procuring an Invitation

Introduction of EFT to relevant Staff

Staff Training (Including guide)

Preparing to Work in a Classroom
(Including lesson themes)

Conclusion & Next Steps.

Bringing EFT into Schools.

Having spent over 30 years working in education, I am well aware of the need for a process to attain emotional freedom. This applies as much to the adults involved as it does to the students.

My previous book, "EFT for Children," was developed as a result of my experience of working in schools. I saw children struggle on a daily basis under the weight of emotional problems and at that time I did not have an adequate tool with which to help them. Teaching and support staff brought their own individual burdens to the emotional mix, resulting in an environment that was frequently less than educational for many students.

Modern education places a great many expectations on those in schools or other educational institutions. Governments set targets which must be met under pain of being labelled "Failing". It therefore falls to the whole school community to ensure success.

Looking back to a period as recently as the late 1980s in the UK, educational institutions were free to set their own curriculum. Teachers had the autonomy to decide what the students most needed to learn and the best approach to employ with any particular group. Without becoming embroiled in the politics, which is not the remit of this work, it is fair to say that a substantial transformation in education provision took place between the late 1980s and mid 1990s. Among the changes experienced at this time was the imposition by Government of a very prescriptive and detailed curriculum. The envisaged outcome of this initiative was a more streamlined approach at a national level. To attain this synchrony across schools, all education providers were required to undergo relevant training, regardless of previous experience or qualification.

By the mid 1990s "The National Curriculum" was legally embedded within the structure of all 5-16 state schools in the UK and its effectiveness was being measured through inspections and testing.

Although school inspections have virtually always been part of the fabric of education, the renewed rigour of OFSTED inspections, while having many positive outcomes, effectively changed the nature of provision, removing much of the inherent joy of teaching and learning as schools strove to maintain copious quantities of evidence.

Among the positive aspects to emerge was the early identification of learners who struggled to attain the expected levels, and an increase in the resulting interventions available to them. The National Curriculum assigned "levels" which were average for all children at a given age. Children falling below these levels could then be easily identified and placed under observation before being incorporated on the "Special

Needs Register" with specific intervention programmes available to them where finances allowed.

At this time the Government also introduced "Emotional Literacy" as part of the curriculum and many schools adopted "SEALS – Social and Emotional Aspects of Learning".

While this in itself was an admirable addition, my experience of the programme was that it was given short timed slots two or three times a year. That is to say that it was treated as another curriculum subject rather than as an ongoing and vital part of everyday interaction.

In effect, while the intention was to enable children to deal effectively with emotional stresses, this did not prove to be the outcome. I would suggest that this was because of emotional literacy not being given the commitment, prominence or regularity needed to have the desired effect.

One of the less positive results of the past twenty five years of Government oversight of education has been the huge burden of stress placed on staff and students alike. Teachers often find themselves in a position of delivering a one-size-fits-all curriculum, albeit at differentiated levels, to classes of up to thirty pupils without other adult support. This situation has clear stress factors for all concerned.

As recently as January 2010 the Teacher Support Network reported that around 10% of all teacher absence for the previous year was due to

> "Mental health reasons, including stress."

Given the huge range of expectations from a variety of sources now being placed on teachers and support staff it is little wonder that these people are crumbling under such weight and are now seeking professional help on an unprecedented scale. The majority of my individual clients work in education!

Unfortunately no such figures exist to indicate the variety of ways in which students are affected by stress. It is often parents who witness the effects through their child's reluctance to attend school, refusal to eat, temper tantrums and so on. In some cases it is easier to label a child as having "behaviour problems" rather than to take a more comprehensive approach to discovering the cause.

Education institutions are already aware of the need for work/life balance and as mentioned, most schools promote emotional literacy and Social and Emotional Aspects of Learning. However, it is my opinion that these measures, despite being well intentioned, do not go far enough to address the growing trend of inability to cope with outside pressure to succeed.

It is from this premise that the need for self care interventions becomes glaringly obvious. When whole school staffs are aware of emotional literacy and know the appropriate tools with which to approach emotional blockages, the whole organisation will benefit.

"Emotional Freedom Techniques" provides exactly such a tool. Its many and varied applications can be used to address the full spectrum of limiting behaviours thereby allowing the organisation to function at optimal levels.

Procuring an Invitation

As already suggested, schools are overwhelmed with new proposals for improvement and the pace of expected change is often breathtaking. It is therefore understandable that, however revolutionary or appropriate a technique for improvement may prove to be, unless legally imposed, it is much less likely to be easily incorporated within the existing framework. This is not to say that schools are closed to new ideas and approaches. Indeed the opposite is more frequently true as demonstrated by the unfailing dedication of most staff members in their efforts to secure the best possible provision for their students. However, within the relatively closed environment of education, the adoption of something as far outside of the usually accepted parameters as EFT, may not immediately be considered.

The initial challenge, then, is in raising awareness.

EFT is such an adaptable tool that it can be difficult to encapsulate its benefits to schools in a concise way. It is imperative that it is not presented as a "cure-all" and indeed it is necessary to minimise the proposed uses of EFT to make it is an acceptable size for consideration.

In the light of this need it is good to focus on a particular area that would give school populations the greatest immediate benefit and value for money.

Some of the most obvious of these might be:

- ➢ Work-Life balance for staff
- ➢ Overload & Stress
- ➢ Behaviour problems
- ➢ Special Needs
- ➢ Difficult home backgrounds
- ➢ Examination nerves
- ➢ Friendship difficulties
- ➢ Self esteem

Gaining an invitation into a school to make an initial presentation may be accomplished through several optional routes.

- You could approach your child's school and ask for an interview with the Head Teacher and/or SENCo (Special Educational Needs Co-Ordinator)

- Select some schools within your area and send a flyer giving an outline of how they would benefit from your services with EFT.

- Having explained your expertise to the Head teacher, ask for permission to address parents meetings.

- All schools have links to Local Education Authority personnel. Find out who is acting on behalf of the focus school and present your proposal to them.

- Create a link with the school nurse/doctor/other medical staffs who visit the school explaining the benefits of EFT and ask that he/she mention your service to relevant school staff.

- Approach a teacher you know and ask about the school's behaviour or Special Needs Policy. You may also request copies of these.

- Propose your own research for a post graduate course, naming Special Needs as your focus. This will involve doing case studies.

- Contact teacher Unions explaining your work and ask for introductions to schools.

- Contact the NAHT or appropriate Head teacher's Union and offer to do a demonstration/give a talk about EFT and its uses and benefits in schools.

These are just some of the ways to "get through the door" of a school. Once inside the onus is on you to promote EFT in an exciting and desirable way, clearly outlining how much more efficiently the school will run when everyone within the community of the school is able to manage their emotional burdens.

In Summary.

- Before bringing EFT into schools you need to know who has responsibility for this area of learning.

- You should be aware of the bridges that already exist within the school structure.

- You need to organise an introduction/training for relevant staff

- You will need to consider parental involvement and how to deliver awareness.

- Because EFT is so varied in its application it has to be minimised for an initial introduction in schools.

- It is usually best to approach EFT through the Special Needs route so those involved will be the Head Teacher and Special Needs Co-ordinator (SENCo)

- Other staff members and Teaching Assistants will help deliver EFT

- School staffs are overwhelmed with expectations from a variety of sources so it is vital that you establish the range of links already in place.

    These include:-

  - ➤ SEALS (Social and Emotional Aspects of learning)
  - ➤ PSHE (personal, social and health education)
  - ➤ IEPs (Individual Education Plans)
  - ➤ Work/Life Balance
  - ➤ Behaviour Policy
  - ➤ Science lessons
  - ➤ Pastoral Care

Introduction of EFT to Head teacher and SENCo

The initial introduction to EFT should necessarily be fairly brief and include a demonstration.

One of the ways that I have introduced EFT to Head teachers is through the Special/Additional Needs route.

To accomplish this I firstly outlined what EFT is, how and when it was discovered and some of its uses.

Very early in the meeting I invited those present to scan their bodies for discomfort and to rate the level. This was followed by some rounds of tapping and re-evaluation. My findings were usually that a significant reduction in discomfort was experienced. This raised the interest level in what else EFT could do.

One of the best demonstrations, done in a fun and light way, is the chocolate addiction. It is always worth explaining here that this process in no way eliminates a person's occasional liking for chocolate but simply replaces the addiction with control.

At this stage you will have set the scene for widening the uses of EFT within the school setting.

Now you can begin to examine how staff would be able to use EFT in classes, with groups or individually. This sets the implication that staff will need training and that particular discussion can take place before the meeting is over.

It is important to show how EFT will benefit all concerned and some anecdotal evidence can be used as a starting point.

My own experience of working in schools has given me a useful databank of situations, some of which are included here. For confidentiality schools and individuals are not named but I have the evidence for their authenticity.

School 1. Having completed a staff introduction I was asked to work with a full class to show how EFT could be used in a general (borrowing benefits) way with all children. This lesson will be revisited at a later stage when looking at plans.

On a follow-up occasion I was asked to work with a child of about 8 years who was experiencing an eating difficulty. With a teaching assistant in attendance to monitor the session, I had the child tap all around sight, smell, taste and texture of different foods. We talked about favourite foods and how and where we like to eat.

It was on talking about the safety of foods that I realised there was a hesitation. It turned out that the child had had a choking experience and Mum had not been present. Since that time it had only become safe to eat if Mum was there. This opened up the possibility for many rounds of tapping on

Recognising the body's need for food,

Comparison with trying to run a vehicle without fuel,

That was then and this is now,

"What if" tapping,

Opening to the possibility that it is now safe to eat

And choosing to feel safe around food.

The outcome of this session was that the child began to eat normally immediately following the intervention and has continued to do so.

School 2.

In this school I was asked by a parent, who had secured LEA funding, to work individually with her son as he had been diagnosed with Dyslexia and Asperger's Syndrome.

Initially I introduced the work through the already familiar series of Brain Gym exercises, creating a bridge between the known and the new.

This child is a boy of 12 years old. I work with "John" for an hour a week within the school setting but on a 1-1 basis.

He happily follows the energy clearing routines and finds many amusing phrases while tapping. Since I have been working with "John" his SAT levels have increased well beyond expectation and his parents credit EFT with the dramatic improvement.

Introduction for Head teacher & SENCo

The following pages give a suggested format for use in working with a management team within school.

I have devised this simple introduction and have used it successfully in a variety of situations including, but not limited to, schools.

I freely give permission for the whole or part of the presentation to be used to bring EFT into schools provided the source is acknowledged.

There are several ways in which this can be utilised:-

- o Create a Power point (This works better with larger audiences)
- o Print, number and laminate the sheets to use in your talk.
- o Make a booklet from the information.
- o Save a copy for reference in your talks.
- o Personalise the presentation to make it your own.

What is EFT?

- EFT is Emotional Freedom Techniques.

- These are techniques which enable you to attain freedom from the emotional negativity associated with physical or mental pain.

How Does It Work?

- To understand how EFT works, it is first necessary to recognise that the human body is composed of different "systems"

  - These are the circulatory, respiratory, nervous, muscular/skeletal, endocrine, immune, digestive and genito-urinal.

- For these systems to work in harmony they have to be connected by the Energy System.

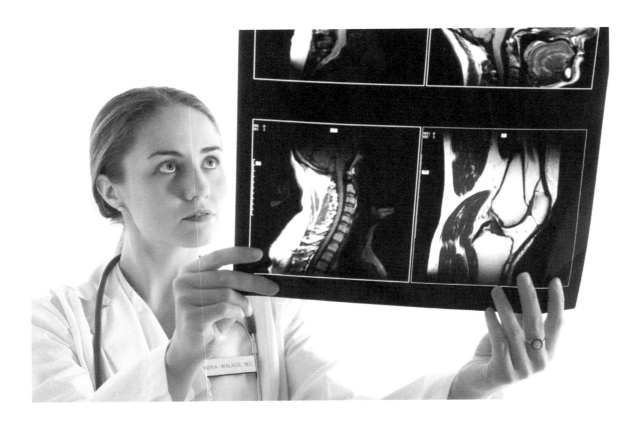

What is this Energy?

- All physical things are composed of energy vibrating at different rates.

- To understand more about the existence of the body's energy systems you can try the following experiment......

Is that my Energy?

- Rub your hands together then begin to move them apart slowly.

- Bring them together and apart several times until you can feel a "pull" between them.

- This is some of the energy from your body.

Body Static

Other experiments might include rubbing a balloon on your hair or shuffling your feet along a carpet. Each will produce static.

For messages to reach the brain from any part of the body there needs to be an energy system along which they travel.

Where is this energy?

- So the energy in the body is like electrical energy.

- It travels round the body along invisible lines called meridians.

- This is also the energy measured in EEG and ECG tests.

Imbalances

EFT is based on the discovery that imbalances in the body's energy system have profound effects on personal psychology.

Energy blocks.

- **The cause of ALL negative emotions is within the body's energy system.**

- Between the distressing memory and the negative emotion is the disruption of the body's energy system

Correction of imbalance.

- Correcting these imbalances can often lead to immediate and lasting relief.

How is EFT carried out?

- EFT is simple to apply and can be carried out in its most basic format by anyone who has a minimum of training.

- The original manual is now available as a book from the website.

- However this is the tip of the iceberg and a much greater application is possible with training.

What do I do?

- Firstly scan your body for any discomfort,

decide what you need to work on and give it a rating out of 10.

  - 1=just noticeable and 10 = unbearable.

- Keep your number in mind so you can measure any changes.

The Set-Up Statement

A typical set-up statement might be something like this:-

"Even though I have this......................

I accept myself" or "I love and value myself" or even simply "I'm ok"

You should feel comfortable with whatever positive statement you make.

The Tapping Points

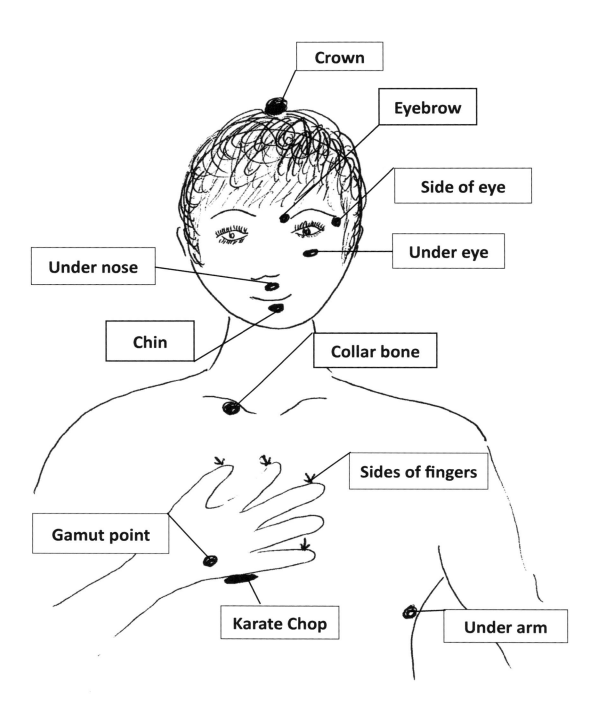

Crown

Eyebrow

Side of eye

Under eye

Under nose

Chin

Collar bone

Sides of fingers

Gamut point

Karate Chop

Under arm

The Sequence

The set-up statement is repeated 3 times while tapping on the

"Karate Chop point"

Once the set-up is complete the statement can be reduced to a reminder phrase.

E.g. if you are working on "this throbbing headache that I get every month" it can be reduced to "This headache" on the points.

Moving on with EFT

Now that we know the basics of EFT, we are ready to move on to some fun ways to make practical use of it.

Let's try some chocolate tasting......

Mmmmm... Chocolate!

First just have a look at the chocolate in front of you.

Decide how much you would like to eat it on a scale of 1-10.

Unwrap and smell it and rerate your desire.

1. Decide on a set-up statement e.g.

   "Even though I MUST have this chocolate........ I love and accept myself"

2. Say your set-up statement 3 times while tapping on the Karate Chop point

3. On all other points, reduce your phrase to "This chocolate"

4. When you have completed one round, reassess your desire. It may have gone up, down or stayed the same. This is ok and does not imply failure.

5. Smell the chocolate again and re-rate the desire.

6. Complete as many more rounds as necessary to get to zero.

7. Congratulations! You are now in control of chocolate!

Next Steps.

This simple demonstration is one way to show an application for EFT.

Within the school setting there are many more ways to utilise it.

You already have the bridges in place i.e. under curriculum guidelines you deliver programmes such as Emotional Literacy, SEALS, Brain Gym, Special Needs interventions and others.

Using the knowledge you now have of EFT can you imagine what applications would be most useful when all staff have relevant training in EFT?

Staff Training.

The process for working with a whole school staff is necessarily much slower and includes more demonstration and practise sessions.

It is effectively a Level 1 training and may be certificated as such if you are a recognised trainer.

It is necessary to point out that level 1 certification only entitles you to work on yourself and with friends and that some study at least of the level 2 materials is required to work publicly.

When staff workshops have been agreed this may take the form of "staff meeting" time (1 hour), a twilight session (2hours) or all or part of a whole day's inset. You need to be clear on which option is available to you depending on the needs of the school. This will inform what you will be able to accomplish in the time. Staff meeting time can only be a brief introduction and it would be best to clarify before agreeing to do this that the material covered will not enable participants to get the best from the programme.

The optimal time would be to have a full day. This must be arranged well in advance as schools have a limited number of training days available to them and these are soon assigned, usually in September, to specific areas of work.

When working with large groups it is always beneficial to have another practitioner with you to take care of any issues that may arise during the practices.

The following outline may be combined with the introduction to Head teachers to give a fuller picture of processes and implementation.

Staff Training/Workshops

My suggestion for working with whole staffs would be to begin the presentation as the introduction. Work through the materials to "The Sequence".

At this point it will be necessary to gauge reaction to the techniques.

Ensure that all participants have worked on a particular problem and given it a level. Ask for their assessment of where the problem is now and continue with further rounds of tapping until resolution or acceptability is reached.

Usually some discussion of the process would follow with questions for clarification.

Before continuing it is worth noting that those involved in education need to know exactly why this process works and where it originated. It is here that I usually include the history and background of EFT. Once its scientific validity is established it is much more acceptable to educators.

A variety of reference materials on hand can add to the weight of evidence for the success of EFT and assure schools that the time taken in the pursuit of this process is of value to them.

Where does EFT originate?

- EFT is both ancient and modern.

- As long as 5000 years ago the ancient Chinese and Japanese understood energy systems and that these energies are carried around the body along the meridians.

- They developed the use of acupuncture.

Acupuncture

- In clearing or interrupting the energy flow with the use of needles the energy was enabled to move more freely and physical or emotional problems could be overcome.

- Think about the acupuncture treatments you have experienced or heard about. They have resolved pain, addictions, phobias etc.

- EFT works in a similar way.

Dr Roger Callahan

During the late 1970s in California Dr Roger Callahan, a clinical psychologist, began studying the body's energy systems.

He discovered that e.g. the stomach meridian has its *end* point just below the eye.

While working with a client he realised that tapping on this end point removed major physical feelings of sickness connected to a water phobia.

Callahan terms his treatment "Thought Field Therapy" because he theorizes that when a person thinks about an experience or thought associated with an emotional problem, they are tuning in to a "thought field." He describes this field as "the most fundamental concept in the TFT system," stating that it "creates an imaginary, though quite real scaffold, upon which we may erect our explanatory notions.

Thought Field Therapy

Further research during the 80s broadened the range of negative emotions covered. This involved detailed study of physiology and an intimate knowledge of where the energy meridians began and ended.

Callahan developed a complicated system of tapping on exactly the right meridian for each client by working out detailed sets of algorithms. His work is published as

"Tapping the Healer Within"

It is known as Thought Field Therapy.

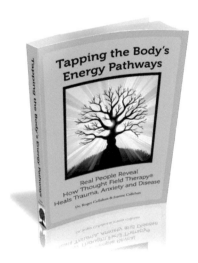

His most recent work was published in February 2011

Gary Craig & EFT

One of Callahan's students, Gary Craig, made the discovery that if a combination of the end points of all the energy meridians was tapped, it was just as effective and the bonus was that you might even relieve blocks other than that being focused on.

Gary Craig is the founder of EFT and for many years he practised and taught EFT techniques around the world.

Craig has recently retired but has enabled much of his work to remain available at

www.eftuniverse.com

Try it out

Unless you experience EFT for yourself, it remains just a theory.

When you teach, you encourage children/students to use all learning styles.

Allow yourself to be open enough to have the same opportunity as you scan your body for any discomfort.

Knowing the background to EFT you may find that this time you are more dedicated to obtaining relief.

Rate the discomfort on a 0-10 scale and let's work on that....................

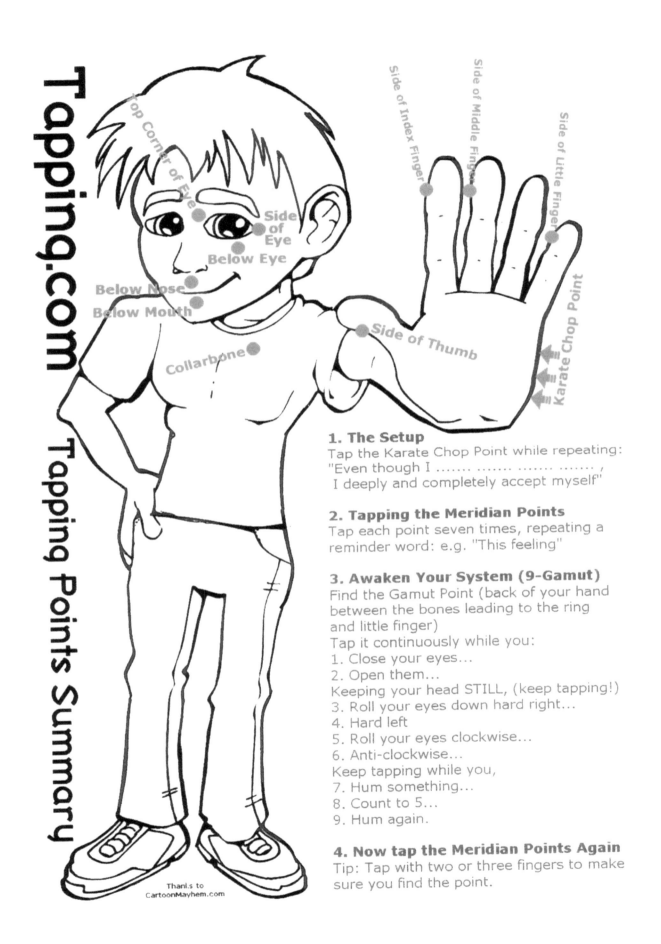

Tapping.com Tapping Points Summary

Top Corner of Eye

Side of Eye

Below Eye

Below Nose

Below Mouth

Collarbone

Side of Index Finger

Side of Middle Finger

Side of Little Finger

Side of Thumb

Karate Chop Point

Thanks to CartoonMayhem.com

1. The Setup
Tap the Karate Chop Point while repeating:
"Even though I ……. ……. ……. ……. ,
I deeply and completely accept myself"

2. Tapping the Meridian Points
Tap each point seven times, repeating a reminder word: e.g. "This feeling"

3. Awaken Your System (9-Gamut)
Find the Gamut Point (back of your hand between the bones leading to the ring and little finger)
Tap it continuously while you:
1. Close your eyes…
2. Open them…
Keeping your head STILL, (keep tapping!)
3. Roll your eyes down hard right…
4. Hard left
5. Roll your eyes clockwise…
6. Anti-clockwise…
Keep tapping while you,
7. Hum something…
8. Count to 5…
9. Hum again.

4. Now tap the Meridian Points Again
Tip: Tap with two or three fingers to make sure you find the point.

How can you use EFT in School?

EFT can be used for a variety of purposes within the classroom. (Including on yourself)

At the beginning of the day you could set up your class for the day's work.

You can use it to break tension;

Remove self limiting thinking;

Overcome negativity;

Deal with hurts (both physical and emotional)

And to come to terms with any day to day negativity associated with difficulty in understanding of given work.

Within Additional Needs EFT has many applications at the group or individual level and these will be explored further at the Class, Group and Individual planning stage.

Further work with Staff.

This would be a good place to demonstrate "Borrowing Benefits"

Ask for a volunteer to work on a particular problem e.g. headache, tension, back pain etc.

Explain that everyone should also have a condition in mind for themselves that they are quietly working on in the background. At the same time they will simply repeat the same phrases and tap the same points as you do.

While focusing on the "client", ask him/her to rate the intensity of their discomfort for later measuring. Everyone present should also rate their discomfort level.

Begin by having all participants do the same set-up statement.

This is followed by some rounds of tapping, using phrases relevant to the focus client, before stopping for re-evaluation. Take time here to allow the other participants to give feedback on their particular issues. It is this feedback that clearly shows how EFT can be useful in large groups. For these purposes we are implying use within a classroom.

Continue tapping on the same client's issue until resolution or satisfaction is reached.

Again take feedback and discussion on the process and outcomes.

A general issue to address with all staff is their limiting beliefs about EFT and their ability to use it successfully.

The Umbrella model of a problem.

What might some of the aspects of Anxiety be?

Preparing to work in a classroom.

At this stage you will probably want to address aspects of a problem. I tend to use the umbrella model and having demonstrated one I get suggestions from participants on what might be the aspects of another umbrella problem.

Depending on the depth of your work with school staff you could then move on to having them begin to imagine working with children. I have found that a good way to do this is to ask them to bring to mind a child for whom EFT would be beneficial. Staff know their students extremely well and have little difficulty in "being" a particular student.

Divide the group into pairs and have one person "be" the student and one the practitioner. Now give some time for a session to take place, working through whatever aspects of the student's problems present themselves.

One of the foremost elements of using EFT in schools is to show that children/young people are far more willing to experiment with it than are adults.

For this reason you may be asked to demonstrate the application of EFT within a classroom. My own experience allowed me to agree to lead a whole class in the introduction to and use of EFT. This was watched by some members of staff so that they could get a feel for how the lesson should proceed.

There is no real reason why you need to be or to have been a teacher to do this. Simply treat the students as you would any other group of people to whom you introduce EFT. The only difference is the age appropriate use of language.

The following pages are taken directly from my book

"Emotional Freedom Techniques for Children". (Author House)

These provide several themes that can be used in working with young people.

Although designed for use with younger children, the material can easily be adapted for older audiences.

This is also the basis of working with whole classes, groups or individuals.

You are Energy!

Your body is made up of energy, flowing round and round.

Some people call this energy "Chi" or "Ki".

It is just like electricity and it gives your body POWER.

The energy flows through invisible lines called MERIDIANS.

If the energy is flowing well and freely, you will feel well and happy.

I can feel my Energy!

You can't see your energy but here is a little experiment to help you to feel it.

- Rub your hands together very fast until they are warm.

- Next, hold your hands in front of you with the palms facing each other.

- Then begin to move your hands slowly apart and back near each other.

- Do this a few times until you can feel the energy like a ball in your hands.

- Play with your energy ball, moving it up and down, in and out.

This shows you your own energy. Just imagine how much energy is in your whole body if that little bit came from your hands!

BUT

Sometimes the energy gets stuck and it can't move freely.

Then you feel scared or sad or angry or even ill.

How can you fix it?

Look at this poem that tells you about the energy and later we will find out how to open up those lines of energy so that you can feel happy again.

Inside my body energy flows

Where it comes from, nobody knows

When it gets stuck, I always feel down

From the tips of my toes right up to my crown.

But now I know just what I can do

If you join in you can learn it too

I tap on the points that set it free

And then I feel yum, That's the key!

Now we need to learn how to tap on the points to set the blocked energy free.

We call these points **"The Happy Tappy Buttons"**

Let's find out where they are and how to use them.

The Happy Tappy Buttons

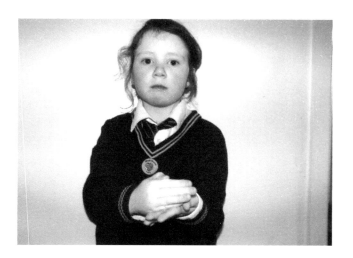

The Karate Chop.

When you have a problem the first thing to do is to set it up to be karate chopped. This is on the part of your hand that you would use to karate chop something. Tap this part of your hand while you set your problem up. This is the Set-up.

The Eyebrow.

This is right at the start of your eyebrow.

The Side Brow.

On this one you tap at the outside edge of your eyebrow.

The High Cheek.

This is on the bone just below your eye.

The Nose.

This one is just below your nose and above your top lip.

The Chin

Now you are tapping between your chin and your bottom lip.

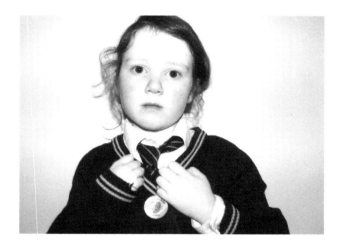

Tarzan.

This one is fun to do. Just thump your chest like Tarzan!

The Monkey.

This one is fun too. Tap under your arm like a monkey.

The Big Top

The last one is right on top of your head. It's like the Big Top of the circus tent and it is the place where you put your happy thoughts at the end of your tapping rounds.

Your "**Yum-Yuck**" card.

You will know when your energy is not flowing well because you will feel sad or angry or upset or just "yuck".

To help you to show how you feel, you can make a "yum-yuck" card like the one shown.

You can move the pointer to the section of the card that shows how you are feeling right now about your problem.

Your first exercise.

- ✓ Close your eyes and let your mind travel round your body.

- ✓ Is there anywhere that you think there might be a block in the energy?

- ✓ Now decide how much of the energy is being blocked. If it's really bad, it will be yuck, If it's no problem, it's yum.

- ✓ Show that on your card.

- ✓ Next put the card down and let's decide how to say what the problem is.

- ✓ Even though you have this problem, it's just an energy block and you are still the same great person you have always been.

- ✓ Set these words up for a karate chop.

- ✓ So we begin by saying "Even though I feel......................... I am still a great person and I'm ok.

Your "Yum/Yuck" card.

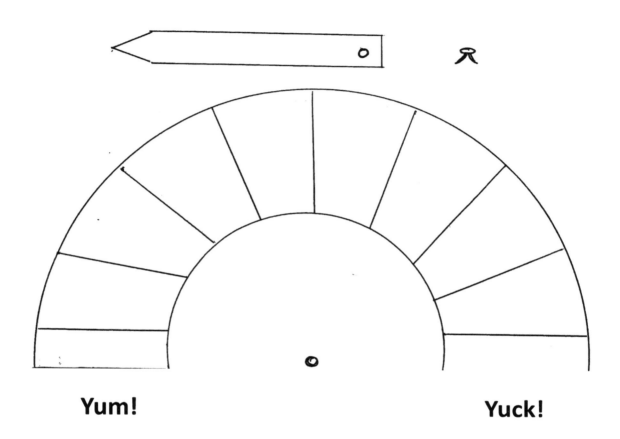

Yum!   **Yuck!**

You can copy this shape onto card and cut it out.

Join the pointer to the card with a split pin. You can colour your card if you want to. Put your favourite colour on the Yum side and a colour you are not so keen on at the Yuck side.

Now you are ready to use it.

The Happy Tappy Points.

- ➢ **Eyebrow**. Tap 5 or 6 times on the part of your eyebrow nearest to your nose and say "I feel.................."

- ➢ **Side brow.** Tap 5 or 6 times on the outside edge of your eyebrow and say "I feel..............................."

- ➢ **High Cheek.** Do the same again on the bone at the top of your cheek and say again "I feel..........................."

- ➢ **Under Nose.** Do the same again

- ➢ **Chin.** Same again

- ➢ **Tarzan.** Same again

- ➢ **Monkey.** Same again

- ➢ **Big Top.** Same again

It's easy, isn't it?

That's one round completed. If there is still some blocking going on, just do the whole round again but this time say "Even though I still feel a bit of this................... it's just some blocked energy and I'm still a great person."

Then when you tap the Happy Tappy Buttons say "This bit of...................."

The BIG Blocks ~
1. Anger.

Sometimes we get great big blocks in our energy.

One of the biggest blocks is when we are angry.

Lots of things or people can make us feel angry.

What things or people make YOU angry?

You might say something like:

- "I get angry when my friend won't play with me."

                                    Or

- "I feel mad when I don't get my own way."
- "I am cross when I have to get up in the morning."
- "Nobody listens to me!"
- "I'm cross because it's not fair that.........."

Everybody gets angry sometimes!

How does Anger make you feel?

What can you feel happening in your body when you are angry? What do you do?

- Do you burn up with rage?
- Do you scream and shout?
- Do you run away and hide?
- Do you feel ugly inside and out?
- Do you feel as if all of you is stuck inside your head?

These are NOT good feelings. You wouldn't want to always feel like this, would you?

Well, you don't have to!
Now you have a choice!

Remember that anger creates a big block in your energy. And big blocks stop you being happy.

Let's laser this anger!

Laser the ANGER!

First of all use your "Yum/Yuck" card to show how strong your anger is right now.

Now we need to set up our self talk on the Karate chop.

"Even though I feel really angry because.....................................
and I could cry/scream/shout, I am still a great person and I'm ready to put this anger down."

Say this 3 times while tapping on the Karate chop.

Now begin to tap the Happy Tappy Buttons as you say,

 "This anger."

Start with the Eyebrow, then Side brow, High cheek, Nose, Chin, Tarzan, Monkey, and Big Top.

When you finish one round, go back to your "Yum/Yuck" card and show if the anger has moved down a bit.

If you were REALLY angry you might need to go round once more or even a few times more!

Just for fun, when the anger has gone, try to get mad about the same thing. Bet you can't!

The BIG Blocks~
2. Worry.

What would it be like if you never had to worry?

EVERYBODY worries about things. Some people worry a lot but others don't seem to worry much at all.

Do you worry a lot or a little? What do you worry about?

Have you ever known a time when worrying made something better?

The problem is that even though we know that worrying never helps, we still do it!

Wouldn't it be great if we could stop ourselves right at the beginning of our worrying?

Guess what! WE CAN!

Wave the worry Goodbye!

As before, think about a big worry that you have.

Give it a level on your "Yum/Yuck" card.

Remember to keep that worry in your head while we work it out.

Next set up your self- talk on the Karate chop.

"Even though I am worried sick that…………………………………… I know that my worrying will make no difference to what happens and I want to free my energy flow and put this worry away. I am still a great person and I am already free."

Now tap on each of the Happy Tappy Buttons and say

"This worry."

Some tricks to learn.

Because worries can be very big we can try another trick to send the worry on its way.

As you go round the Tappy Buttons a second time, put different words about the worry on each one, like this......

Eyebrow ~ "This really big worry"

Side brow ~ "It's too heavy for me to carry."

High Cheek ~ "I'm ready to leave it behind."

Nose ~ "I know things will work out anyway."

Chin ~ "I have no need to worry about this."

Tarzan ~ "Somebody else can do the worrying if they want."

Monkey ~ "I've finished with it."

Big Top ~ "Now I choose to be free."

Now, show on your "Yum/Yuck" card how you feel about that old worry.

The BIG blocks ~
3. Fear.

Fear is a bit like a big worry.

We are all afraid sometimes. We can have really BIG fears or our fears can be quite small. We don't need to carry fear around because it blocks our energy.

What are you afraid of?

You might be afraid of the dark or afraid of dogs or spiders or another animal. You might be afraid that you or someone in your family will be poorly. Some people are afraid of new situations or of meeting someone they don't know.

There are hundreds of things we could be afraid of if we really think about it.

But why be afraid when we can do something about it?

Fade the Fear!

- First of all, think about the fear you want to fade.

- Next we set it up on the karate chopping block.

- On the karate chop we might say something like..............
"Even though I have this fear of.. I am still a great person and I really like myself."

- Say this 3 times while tapping the karate chop point.

- Now work your way around all the Happy Tappy Buttons saying on each "This fear."

- When you get round once, have another look at the fear and see if it has faded a bit.

- If it has, go round again until you don't feel afraid of that same thing any more.

- If your fear is still as big as ever, you can try the tricks you learned in the last chapter.

- On each Tappy Button you can say something about the fear like this....................

Tricks to Fade the Fear.

- "This big fat fear that keeps me awake at night"

- "This fear that is just blocking my energy"

- This fear about.........................."

- I don't need to carry this fear any more"

- I have no more use for this fear"

- This fear that started when I............................"

- I choose to be free of this fear"

- I choose to be happy and free"

Always end at the Big Top with a happy statement.

The BIG blocks ~
4. I'm Not Good Enough!

How often have you felt as if you were not good enough?

Even grown-ups feel like this sometimes.

Maybe someone has made you feel not good enough, a friend, a parent, a teacher or someone else, or maybe you did it to yourself by imagining that you should be better than you are at certain things.

Think about a time when you felt like everybody was better than you. Did someone call you an unpleasant name? How did you feel inside? What happened in your body?

You probably didn't realise it at the time but you had just allowed a big block to stop your energy flowing freely.

The problem is that those blocks stay there until you tap them free. Let's do that now.

Free the Flow.

- Begin by calling to mind the biggest time when you felt not good enough. Think about who was there, why you weren't good enough, what was said and so on.

- Show on your "Yum/Yuck" card how strong the feeling is at this moment.

- Now think of a good way to describe that feeling for the karate chop block.

- You might say something like.. . "Even though I always feel as if I'm no good at Maths I know I'm still a great person and there is nobody like me in the whole world."

- Use words that fit how YOU feel rather than just following the words in the book.

- So, with the problem on the karate chop, remember to say it 3 times.

- Now you are ready to really free the flow!

- On each of the Happy Tappy Buttons you just need to say **"This not good enough feeling"**

- It is a good idea to go round again just to make sure before you examine the feeling again to see if it has come nearer to the "Yum" on your card

I AM good enough!

Feeling not good enough is a VERY BIG block so you may need to use the extra tricks again. Try this...............................

- When you are putting the problem on the karate chop block, see if you can be really clear about what it was that made you feel not good enough.

- Use those exact words to describe the problem...............
"Even though my friend said you're not very good at this game" or "Even though I tried my best but I still couldn't do it" or "Even though everybody else was able to swim a whole length and I couldn't"

- Remember to always finish the sentence with "I'm still a great person and I like myself or there's no-one else like me."

- Now, on the Happy Tappy Buttons you can put words from your problem like this..........................

- "I wasn't good enough, I tried my best, my friend said, I wanted to get it right, I am good at lots of things, there is no-one else quite like me, and so on.

- Make sure that you put something good on the Big Top!

The BIG Blocks~
5. Sadness.

Have you ever been really sad about something?

Things happen in our lives which make us feel so sad that we think we are all alone in our sadness. It doesn't have to be like this. Each day we have many choices to make and everything that happens allows us to make new choices.

Maybe you have felt sad because your friend wouldn't play or because you lost something or maybe you have had a BIG sadness like you feel when a person or a pet you knew has died.

Maybe we need to experience a bit of sadness sometimes so that we can appreciate the happiness.

If you knew that you could choose to be happy instead of sad, would you choose happiness?

Solve the Sadness Problem.

By now you will have a good idea of how to decide how strong the feeling is using your "Yum/Yuck card and how to set up your problem on the karate chop and to tap it down on the Happy Tappy Buttons. Here's a reminder.

❖ How strong is your sadness? Show it on your card.

❖ Think of a good way to describe your problem e.g "Even though I feel really sad that my cat died, I am still a great person and I love myself."

Or

"Even though I feel so sad that I could cry for a week and I don't even know why I feel this way, I am still a great person and I love myself."

❖ Set the problem up 3 times on the karate chop.

❖ Now work around the Happy Tappy Buttons saying, "This sadness."

❖ You might go round twice before you stop to see if the sadness has moved down nearer to "Yum".

❖ If you are a lot happier now, you can choose to stop but if you need to carry on then use the special tricks like this.......

....

Solve the Sadness Problem Even More.

- Start as you did before by working out how strong the sadness is now and showing it on your card.

- Set the sadness up on the karate chop using words that are meaningful to you.

- Say your set up statement 3 times.

- Next, put some of your statement words on to each of the Buttons as you tap.

- It might be something like this...

  Eyebrow: "I feel so sad"

  Side brow: "This sadness weighs me down."

  High cheek: "Nobody understands my sadness"

  Nose: "I wonder what it would be like to change this sadness into happiness."

  Chin: "Maybe it would be ok for me to leave the sadness behind.

  Tarzan: "I WILL leave the sadness behind.

  Monkey: "I choose to leave the sadness behind and I choose to be happy"

  Big Top: "I am happy and free."

- You can always go round again using the same or new words until you really do feel happy.

- When you finish it is a good idea to test your work by trying to feel the same way you did before about that same thing.

The BIG Blocks ~
6. Guilt.

Do you think there is anyone in the whole world that has never done anything wrong?

EVERYBODY has made a wrong choice at some time.

How you feel about that choice depends on what you do about it.

Maybe it is not something that you can put right very easily so it might be that you just end up feeling guilty because you knew better but still made the choice.

Do you have to hold on to and carry that guilt around with you for the rest of your life? NO, you don't!

Here's why.

Having you feel guilty does not help anyone else, even the person you made the wrong choice about.

All it does is BLOCK your ENERGY.

Gunning for Guilt.

So let's get that guilt out. You know how to check its strength and how to do the set-up and tapping by now. Here it is again.

- Decide how strong the guilt is and show that on your card.

- Decide how best to describe what your guilt feels like. It might be something like... It feels like a big heavy weight on my shoulders.............. or This guilty feeling makes me really uncomfortable..... or I feel bad in my chest because I did this.......................

- Choose whatever sounds most like the way you feel and use that as your set-up statement.

- "Even though I have this big heavy weight in my chest because I feel guilty that................................. I am still a great person and I still like/love myself."

- Say your set-up 3 times while tapping on the karate chop.

- For the first round you only need to say "This guilty feeling" on the Happy Tappy Buttons.

- When you have gone round twice, check how strong the feeling is now.

Tricks for Guilt.

Because guilt is usually quite strong, you will probably need to use the extra tricks to get it right down.

Remember that all you need to do is to put some of your words on each of the Tappy Buttons as you go round.

You can use the same set-up statement as before.

It might come out something like this......................................

- "Even though I am still feeling a bit guilty about............. I know I was doing what I thought was best at the time and I love myself in spite of sometimes being wrong."

- Eyebrow:- "I made a wrong choice"

- Side brow:- "I am sorry for choosing the wrong thing"

- High cheek:- "I was doing what I had to at that time"

- Nose:- "I know how to make good choices"

- Chin:- "That time is past now and I choose to be free of that guilt"

- Tarzan:- "I am always improving"

- Monkey:- "I am able to see how my actions can affect other people"

- Big Top:- "I choose to be free and to allow other people to be free too."

EFT for Everything.

Well done! Now you know how to get rid of all those energy blocks.

We have read about and worked with ways to end fear, worry, guilt, sadness and not being good enough.

Now you are ready to really use your imagination!

You can use EFT for ANY problem, no matter how big or how small. It's the same routine for everything.

- Give your problem a level from 1-10.

- Set it up on the Karate Chop.

- Go round the Tappy Buttons saying the name of the problem.

- Go round again, just to make sure.

- Check the level again and if it's not gone use some of the extra tricks we tried before.

Happy Tapping!

Conclusion and Next Steps.

We all look forward to the day when everyone has the skills to manage their own emotional wellbeing. EFT is one of the most efficient and effective tools for this purpose. If we can begin at "grassroots" level, with our children and young people, it could be an easy step to realising this freedom for all.

It is within the hands of practitioners everywhere to spread the word and the ability throughout education systems.

As mentioned briefly in the introduction, unless schools are required to follow a particular theme within the curriculum, it is less likely to be given the attention required to be as effective as possible. Therefore our aim must be to get adequate recognition through the channels holding the power of persuasion.

The ultimate objective would be to attain Government validation and in this way to have EFT in schools as a required initiative. This can be a slow process and would initially need to show efficiency and effectiveness. For this to happen it would be necessary to have an abundance of case studies.

Many places of education are already open enough to take whatever steps are required to attain a platform for optimum learning and it is these forward thinking bodies that can provide the basis for validation of EFT.

What is immediately required is sufficient schools using EFT and getting emotional freedom for their students to be widely publicised in local and national newspapers.

Influential bodies in this respect can be

- Members of Parliament,

- Teacher support agencies,

- Teacher Unions,

- Local Education Authorities,

- Head Teacher Unions,

- Doctors/Nurses,

- Newspaper editors,

- Parent groups,

- Governing Bodies,

- Radio/TV Presenters

- And indeed anyone who has an interest in the education system.

I wish you peace and healing.

"Every human being is the author of their own health or disease"—Buddha.

CPSIA information can be obtained
at www.ICGtesting.com
Printed in the USA
259061LV00006B